T0195801

In Search of the Universal Christ

A Paradigm Shift in
Christian Beliefs

Paul A. Chimzar

WESTBOW
PRESS®
A DIVISION OF THOMAS NELSON
& ZONDERVAN

WestBow Press books may be ordered through booksellers or by contacting:

WestBow Press
A Division of Thomas Nelson & Zondervan
1663 Liberty Drive
Bloomington, IN 47403
www.westbowpress.com
844-714-3454

ISBN: 978-1-6642-9883-5 (sc)
ISBN: 978-1-6642-9882-8 (e)

Library of Congress Control Number: 2023908188

Print information available on the last page.

WestBow Press rev. date: 05/02/2023

CONTENTS

CHAPTER 1

INTRODUCTION

I have been on my spiritual journey most of my life. At a young age, I wanted to be loved by God and feel his presence. I was born into a Roman Catholic family in the late fifties before Vatican II. My parents were devoted Catholics. We went to church every Sunday and attended on Holy Days too. My mother was a former teacher and was my Catechism teacher from first through third grades. I had my first confession. It wasn't called "reconciliation" back then. We went to confession every Saturday. I remember going to confession several times and making up sins so I would have something to confess. I had my first communion. I was an altar boy for many years. I went through confirmation class in ninth grade and was confirmed. For confirmation class, they used the old *Baltimore Catechism* book. My religious beliefs were formed during first through ninth grade using pre–Vatican II teachings. I was taught to believe that

- we were born with original sin;
- Jesus died for our sins;
- God was judging and punitive, but merciful (*God keeps score*);
- committing a sin was shameful and would prevent us from going to heaven;
- only "good" boys and girls go to heaven;

- we should live lives of reason, for our emotions will lead to sin;
- we must be loyal and faithful to the Catholic Church (*we must not become too involved with "those" Protestants*);
- we should work toward going to heaven by avoiding sin and doing "good" works;
- heaven is a place "up there;" and
- in church, we were told what to believe and what not to believe.

After I was confirmed, a small group of classmates and I were disappointed that the Catholic Church did not provide a path for spiritual growth going forward after confirmation. We formed a group and found a Catholic couple to sponsor us. We met once or twice a month. My key takeaways from the group experience were (1) be a loyal Catholic, (2) continue to learn and practice your faith by following the doctrine and teachings of the church, (3) do good works, and (4) pray. There was no discussion about a spiritual journey in Christ or developing an experiential relationship with God. From this experience, I moved on, seeking more.

In college, I took a class through the Catholic Newman Center to acquire a deeper understanding of the Catholic faith after Vatican II. The class used Anthony Wilhelm's *Christ Among Us*. This book provided a thorough, up-to-date discussion of Catholic theology, traditions, and practices after Vatican II for new Catholics and those returning to the faith. Once again, I learned a lot about the doctrine and teachings of the Catholic Church, but I learned nothing about a spiritual journey in Christ. It was all about knowledge gathering, then how to develop a relationship with God. I still was hungry for a relationship with God and not satisfied with just "knowing" about him.

After college, I took an engineering job in a manufacturing plant in Iowa for a global manufacturing company. I was asked by the priest of the Catholic church I attended if I would be interested in participating in their RCIA (Rite of Christian Initiation of Adults) program. I agreed and started attending RCIA classes. During the second class, I met my future wife and became her sponsor. I was very excited and proud to be her sponsor throughout the process. She became a Catholic at the Easter vigil. She and I were married in the same Catholic church by the same priest about a year and a half later. Once again, the RCIA classes were about discussing Catholic theology, traditions, and practices for new Catholics and those returning to the faith; they were not about the journey.

Throughout my early life, I participated in a couple of spiritual retreats at my church. None of them sparked an experiential relationship with God. I even studied and participated in the Q'ero shamanism spiritual practices with a friend. The Q'ero are indigenous people of the Andes Mountains in Peru. Through the Q'ero shamanism, I began to learn about spiritual rituals that help in a person's spiritual journey, and how the spiritual rituals help make the spiritual journey more experiential than cerebral.

In my late forties, I attended a men's spiritual retreat at my Catholic church. The visiting priest and retreat leader talked about the spiritual journey that men take throughout the stages of their lives. We were encouraged to share our personal stories about our spiritual journeys. I don't remember if anyone shared. However, I do remember the answer the retreat leader gave when asked, "Is there a road map or process that we can use to facilitate our spiritual journeys?"

I was shocked and disappointed by his answer. He said, "Yes! The Twelve-Step Program." (The Twelve-Step Program was founded in 1935 by two alcoholics, Bill Wilson and Dr. Robert Holbrook Smith, in Akron, Ohio. It is used extensively to help recovering addicts.)

My reaction to his answer was, "After two thousand years of existence, the Catholic Church does not have its own road map or process to facilitate a person's spiritual journey? Really!" I became very disillusioned with the Catholic Church because of this retreat.

My childhood was very painful and lonely. I grew up with two sisters. I was the oldest. My dad was a loud, rageful alcoholic who was emotionally and verbally abusive to us. My mother was the submissive, emotionally detached wife. During her lifetime, she didn't ever hug or hold us children once. I felt emotionally neglected by my father and mother.

My dad resented me throughout his life for what his father said to him about me. When I was born, his father, my grandfather, said that he "would die for me," which really hurt my father. My dad was the youngest in his family, and I got the sense that he wasn't exactly planned and wanted by his parents. My dad showed no affection or encouragement toward me throughout my childhood. In fact, it was just the opposite: I was the lightning rod for his rage when things went wrong for him.

Because my dad was a rageful alcoholic all the time, I could not have friends over to play or hang out. I had no close friends with whom I felt comfortable sharing my situation and feelings. I was isolated and lonely.

I developed chronic anxiety issues in second grade, which I have carried throughout my life. I was diagnosed with chronic depression after my wife and I had our first child. I have been in psychotherapy (talk therapy) for over thirty years. My symptoms from chronic anxiety and depression have lessened very little. In spite of my mental health issues, I have a successful marriage, have raised two loving, successful children, and have had a successful career.

My life changed with my recent therapist. I will refer to her as Grace to protect her real name. I shared my life story and my struggles with mental illness with Grace. I told her my past therapies did not seem to improve my mental health. After several sessions, Grace told me that I, most likely, was suffering from complex posttraumatic stress disorder (PTSD). She explain what complex PTSD was and why it was difficult to treat. I did my own research on PTSD and found the "talk" therapy was not an effective treatment for complex PTSD.

PTSD is caused by a single traumatic event, such as a tragic war event, car accident, or violent act against a person. Complex PTSD is caused by long-lasting trauma that continues or repeats for months, even years; it is typically the result of childhood trauma. In my case, my father was a loud, rageful alcoholic. His daily routine was to come home from work around 3:30 p.m. and start drinking. By 5:30 p.m., he was drunk and started yelling about anything and everything until he went to bed around 10:30 p.m. He repeated this routine seven days a week, over 350 days a year for fourteen years of my childhood. To give you an idea of the loudness, with the doors and windows of the house shut, you could hear him yelling ten to fifteen feet outside the house. Imagine living in the house and trying to get to sleep.

Besides my father's daily drunken routine, he had a rageful temper that could be unpredictable. Everything and anything could set him off, and I was the target. I was yelled at for all sorts of things, usually not in my control. It was like living in a minefield, never knowing when the next mine would go off.

Six weeks before my high school graduation, my dad's drunken behavior worsened and my mother's ability to cope was finally unraveling. They were yelling at each other for most of the evening. Later I found my mother in the basement crying. I went upstairs, confronted my dad, and told him his drunken behavior had to stop. He was taken back by my anger and forcefulness. Within a few minutes, my dad called his priest and doctor. They immediately came over to discuss a rehab plan for my dad.

Within a day or two, my dad was in an alcohol rehab unit for six weeks. The rehab facility let my dad out for a day to attend my graduation from high school. Of course, he had a rageful episode toward me before the graduation party. I promised myself that I would never live in his house again, and I didn't.

Throughout this difficult childhood, I never truly felt the presence of God, but I sure had a better understanding of the torture, pain, suffering, and isolation that prisoners of war must have felt.

I want to go back to how I found my new therapist, Grace. I read the book *Healing the Unaffirmed: Recognizing Emotional Deprivation Disorder* by Conrad W. Baars, MD, and Anna A. Terruwe, MD. The book opened my eyes to my mother's emotional detachment and unaffirming behavior toward me. The book really struck a chord with me. After reading the book, I began seeking therapists who were familiar with emotional deprivation disorder and made a practice of affirming their patients. I didn't find any therapist locally who treated emotional deprivation disorder and decided take my search nationwide. After a referral from the Baars Institute, I contacted Grace. Grace lived on the east coast. We video conferenced weekly at first and then monthly. She was a good listener and very affirming.

Our patient-therapist relationship grew. Grace shared many resources with me that she felt might help in dealing with my mental illness. She asked if I practiced a faith. I said yes and told her that I was a recovering Catholic. Grace was Catholic too. I described my faith journey and my disappointment in the Catholic Church. Grace listened intently and affirmed my story. She shared her own disappointment in the Catholic Church. During one session, Grace introduced me to Father Richard Rohr's podcasts, which she found refreshing. I listened to several of Father Rohr's podcasts and became hooked on his different perspective of Catholicism. In one of his podcasts, Father Rohr briefly described his new book, *The Universal Christ: How a Forgotten Reality Can Change Everything We See, Hope For, and Believe. The Universal Christ* changed my life and started me on my spiritual journey in Christ.

Over a course of a year, I read the *The Universal Christ* a couple more times. I wanted to share my insights from the book, but had difficulty explaining them to others. I decided to create a picture to help me explain my insights from the book. The depiction of the spiritual growth and transformation journey in Christ is displayed as a picture in Figure 1. The depiction in Figure 1 is the output from reflecting on Father Rohr's book. I strongly recommend and encourage you to read his book to better understand the foundation for the spiritual depiction portrayed in the picture below.

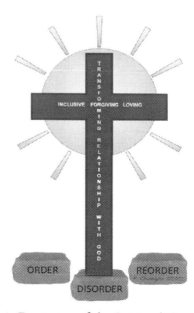

Figure 1: Depiction of the Spiritual Growth and
Transformational Journey in Christ

CHAPTER 2

SEEING WITH NEW EYES

After reading and reflecting on *The Universal Christ*, I had a paradigm shift in my beliefs. I began to see Catholic doctrine and teachings with new eyes. My Christian beliefs shifted from the old Catholic paradigm to a new paradigm—one that included a cosmic, universal Christ. I shifted from my past beliefs to a new set of beliefs. These included shifting

- *from* a view of being born with original sin *to* being born with original goodness;
- *from* the belief that Jesus died for our sins *to* the belief that Jesus Christ died to show God's outpouring love for us and, through his resurrection, transform us into the Body of Christ;
- *from* a view of retributive justice *to* a restorative justice framework;
- *from* seeing a judging, punitive God *to* a loving, forgiving God;
- *from* seeing sin as shameful and something to be avoided *to* seeing sin as a deviation from Christ's path that is a fact of life and provides teaching moments for spiritual growth and transformation;

- *from* a personal, tribal, and exclusive God *to* a universal, cosmic God who includes all things and loves all things, not just earthlings; and
- *from* a goal of working toward going to heaven *to* creating and growing a transforming relationship with God and experiencing heaven on earth.

Let me expand on the first bullet above. The idea of *original sin* was put forth by St. Augustine in the fifth century. Nowhere in the Bible is *original sin* mentioned. In addition, early Christians before the fifth century did not have a reason for conceiving the concept of *original sin*. It is interesting to note that most other world religions have a sense of primal goodness in their creation stories.[1] At the time, the concept of *original sin* helped to define the problem of why sin and suffering existed in the world and why Jesus was the solution. By nature, humans tend to focus on problems and solutions. We have a tendency to look at the world as a problem or a threat to be solved or resolved. Furthermore, humans do not like "not knowing," to the point where we will invent reasons and explanations to lessen the discomfort and fear of uncertainty and ambiguity. The concept of *original sin* may have been helpful in our spiritual evolution, but it has outlived its reasoning and usefulness and now hinders our relationships with a loving God.

Let's take a step back and explore the reason behind the story of the fall of Adam and Eve. We are to believe God placed a sin on all children at birth, because Eve took an apple from the tree of knowledge, gave it to Adam to eat when God had forbidden it. First off, we usually think of sin as a matter of personal responsibility and culpability, something done by us. However, original sin is something done to us. What? This thinking makes God out to be an angry, punitive tyrant and not a loving and forgiving God.

In contrast, *original goodness* means that we are all born in the image of God's goodness, unwoundedness (innocence), and dignity. It

---

[1] Richard Rohr, *The Universal Christ: How a Forgotten Reality Can Change Everything We See, Hope For, and Believe* (New York: Convergent Books, 2019), 61.

is through our life's challenging and hurtful experiences that we become wounded, lose our innocence, and become less trusting of others. We develop egos out of fear and the need for protection from others who may hurt us. We put on masks or facades over our true selves to avoid ridicule and alienation from others. We lose our true selves in all our woundedness. However, God loves our true selves even when we or others do not. The spiritual journey in Christ is simply a matter of becoming who we already are and reclaiming our original goodness.

The first bullet above leads into the second: that *Jesus died for our sins*. Let's explore where this theology came from and ask the question, "Why did Jesus die?" First, we begin with idea of atonement. The definition of *atone* is to make amends, reparation, or compensation for one's mistakes, sins, or wrongdoings toward God or our neighbors. Atonement is defined by *Encyclopedia Britannica* as "the process by which people remove obstacles to their reconciliation with God."[2] With this basis, we can answer the question, "Why did Jesus die?" The prevailing Christian answer is that *Jesus died for our sins.* It is based on the penal substitutionary atonement theory. This theory puts forth that "Jesus, by his own sacrificial choice, was punished in place of us sinners, thus satisfying the 'demands of justice' so that God could forgive our sins. This theory of atonement ultimately relies on another commonly accepted notion—the *original sin* of Adam and Eve, which we were told tainted all human beings."[3] The question is, "Is this true?" Well, in fact, substitutionary atonement theory is just that: a "theory" and not dogma.[4]

Substitutionary atonement theory is a much more recent development than the notion of original sin. Development of atonement theory started in the eleventh century with Anselm of Canterbury, who wrote a paper called *Cur Deus Homo?* (*Why a God Human?*). In addition, it fully relies upon a retributive notion of justice, meaning we need to give restitution or be punished for our sins. If we stop and think about this,

---

2   *Encyclopedia Britannica Online,* s.v. "atonement," accessed March 24, 2023, https://www.britannica.com/topic/atonement-religion.

3   Rohr, *The Universal Christ,* 140.

4   Rohr, *The Universal Christ,* 140.

it makes Jesus's suffering, dying, and resurrecting a one-time transaction between Jesus and his Father as a reparation for our sins. In this light, God is made to be very small indeed. This idea paints God the Father as "a tyrant, a sadist, a rage-aholic dad, or a just an unreliable lover."[5] No wonder some Christians have a problem with trusting and believing in God.

In contrast, the Franciscans, led by John Duns Scotus (1266–1308), refused to see Jesus's incarnation and passion on the cross as a mere transaction for sin. Instead, they believed that the cross dramatically demonstrated God's outpouring love for us. It was meant to literally shock ours being and turn us back to God. Jesus's incarnation and passion are meant to continually transform us through the Eucharist and draw us closer to God and to each other. It is not merely a one-time transaction but a continually transforming relationship with God and with each other.

The third bullet above deals with the notion of justice: retributive versus restorative. In retributive justice, the sinner is punished and/or gives reparations for committing a sin to balance the scales of justice with God. In restorative justice, the sinner is restored to good standing and victim (or victims) is healed through the help of their community.

Retributive justice requires that a law, rule, or commandment be set and enforced. Those in authority created and enforced these laws. If a person breaks the law, then that person is punished based on the severity and extent of the wrongdoing. It is a *quid pro quo* mentality. With retributive justice, a person tends to view the world dualistically as one in which there are only two contrasting, mutually exclusive choices or realities. Retributive justice thinking can lead to seeing God as a tyrant and a punisher. This is contrary to Jesus's teaching of love and forgiveness. Remember, Jesus never punished anyone and neither did his disciples seek retributive justice for Jesus's crucifixion.

In contrast, Jesus taught us to practice restorative justice, to forgive and heal sinners. Jesus was all about forgiving and healing the sinner, and restoring the sinner into the community. There is no room for *quid*

---

5   Rohr, *The Universal Christ,* 139.

pro quo thinking. Christ Jesus wants us to put our focus and energy on building relationships and not on the "law and scales of justice." In a restorative justice perspective, God is seen as loving and forgiving towards all things. Oh! What *good news* this is for all us sinners![6]

What is sin? Sin is defined in my *Baltimore Catechism* as any willful thought, word, deed, or omission contrary to the law of God. It is an offense against God's law. This definition of sin relies heavily on the word *law*. As I discussed earlier, retributive justice requires that the law be set and enforced. Those in authority or in control can create and enforce these laws through reward or punishment. This definition of sin is based on a legalistic approach to Christianity. This approach started with the legalization of Christianity in AD 313 by the Roman emperor Constantine. The Roman Catholic Church adopted the Roman Empire's hierarchical political structure and legal system with considerable influence from Emperor Constantine. For the next 1700 years, the Roman Catholic Church practiced legalism, putting law before the Gospel.

I think that this legalistic approach to sin has led to an authoritative, over-controlling Catholic clergy, who are preoccupied by the sins of the individual and in keeping with the status quo. Obedience and loyalty become the highest virtues within this structure instead of love, communion, or solidarity with God. Legalism in the Roman Catholic Church has led to the practice of shaming, which lessens the dignity of a person. Legalism focuses on our human faults rather than on our goodness. Legalism hinders our ability to create and grow in a transforming relationship with God.

Can we frame sin in a different light? The answer is *yes*! The Hebrew word for sin literally means "to go astray" or "miss the mark." Jesus used the parables of the shepherd and his sheep and the prodigal son to show God's never ending love for us, even when we sin (or deviate from the "path"). God loves us so much that he goes after us when we deviate from the path (sin) and brings us back. What a beautiful thing! Going forward, *sin* can be defined as a deviation from the path towards

---

6   The fourth bullet of the to/from list has been addressed.

a transforming and loving relationship with God and our neighbors. The more we deviate from the "path," the more we need God's help. Sin can become a teaching moment or a lesson learned that provides us opportunities for spiritual growth during our spiritual journeys. It does not need to be a matter of breaking a law and needing to be punished. I don't believe that punishment has led to any long-lasting change in the world. Our US jails and prisons are not less full because of punishment.

Sin is not without its consequences. We need to be held accountable for our actions. God doesn't punish us for our sins;[7] instead, he allows the consequences of our sins to do that. As Father Rohr states, "Humans are punished by their sins more than for their sins."

To address the fifth bullet above, we start with the following basic beliefs about God.

1. God existed before time existed.
2. God is infinite.
3. God consists of three persons: God the Father, Son, and Holy Spirit.
4. God created all things and loves all things.

Most, if not all, Christians agree with these beliefs.

Next, we know that the universe has existed for 13.8 billion years. Humans and their ancestors have been walking the planet for about 6 million years. *Homo sapiens,* the modern form of humans, evolved 300,000 years ago from *Homo erectus.* Human civilizations started forming around 6,000 years ago.[8] Therefore, humans and their ancestors have existed only for four-thousandth of the universe's existence. As vast and old as the universe is, with all of its galaxies, it is hard to believe that we are the only creatures created in God's image, or that God waited 13.74 billion years to create something to love. Did God come only for us earthlings? Take a moment to contemplate this. If you believe

---

[7]   Rohr, *The Universal Christ,* 196.

[8]   Victor Kiprop, "How Long Have Humans Been On Earth?" World Atlas, accessed January 12 2021, https://www.worldatlas.com/articles/how-long-have-humans-been-on-earth.html.

that God created only humans in his image, then you may have an egocentric view of God, a very limited God and not one who is infinite. The true God is much more cosmic, much more universal.

Western Christianity has come to believe in a personal, exclusive, and tribal God. In some cases, certain Christians believe in a personal savior (i.e., Jesus), who will only save them and/or their congregation. As Father Rohr writes, "A merely personal God becomes tribal and sentimental, and a merely universal God never leaves the realm of abstract theory and philosophical principles."[9] Faith in a personal God only leaves one focused on a personal relationship with Jesus and leaves out the bigger relationship with the Body of Christ, in other words, *Christ and our neighbors in the present tense.*

In the United States, where individualism is highly valued, the spiritual journey has become a journey for individuals rather than a journey for the Body of Christ (i.e., a spiritual community, made up of all individuals, who are in solidarity with God and others and believe and follow the teachings of Christ). An individualistic view of the Gospel has "allowed the clergy great control over individual behavior, via rewards and punishments. Obedience to authorities becomes the highest virtue in this framework, instead of love, communion or solidarity with God or others, including the marginalized."[10] Today's Christianity has become more about being a loyal member of an exclusive club than becoming a member of the Body of Christ, which includes everyone, Christians and non-Christians alike.

With new eyes and ears, I started viewing and listening to the Gospel as a member of the Body of Christ. From this view, all are included and no one is excluded. This means non-Christians, such as Jews, Muslims, Buddhists, atheists, and so on, are included in the Body of Christ. This view may be challenging for most. Next, I expanded my belief in Christ; as St. Paul put it, "*There is only Christ. Christ is everything and in everything*" (Colossians 3:11 GW; emphasis added). It took some time for the last sentence to sink in for me. Christ is in

---

[9] Rohr, *The Universal Christ,* 19.
[10] Rohr, *The Universal Christ,* 165.

all people (Christians and non-Christians) and in all things (including everything that is non-human).

Let us explore the last bullet of our list, specifically, the *goal of working toward going to heaven*. Most of us were taught that heaven was up there somewhere and that God would judge us after we die to determine if we are "good enough" to enter heaven. In addition, we were taught to avoid sinning, because sin would prevent us from entering heaven. Only people who were free from sin could enter heaven. This belief is based on a retributive justice framework that was explored earlier. I believe that this belief has led to the practice of shaming others. I strongly felt this growing up as a Roman Catholic. As a side note, this belief has allowed clergy to wield control over their people's actions, via reward and punishment. No wonder there was a Protestant Reformation.

The good news is that there is an alternate perspective based a restorative justice framework. In restorative justice, the sinner is forgiven, healed, and restored to good standing with help of the community. This action is what Jesus asked us to do. Jesus never punished anyone. In this light, no one will be excluded from "being in heaven" unless he or she chooses to be. God always includes and never excludes.

Next, heaven is a state of being and not a place. "Being in heaven" means being fully in union with Christ. The transformational process of getting to the state of "heaven" is called *salvation*. If a person practices salvation, that person will experience moments of "heaven" while alive on earth. "Being in full union with Christ" means being fully human and fully divine like Christ. As Christians, we are called by Christ to follow him. We do this by creating and growing in a transforming and loving relationship with God and experiencing heaven on earth.

CHAPTER 3

THE SPIRITUAL GROWTH AND TRANSFORMATIONAL JOURNEY IN CHRIST

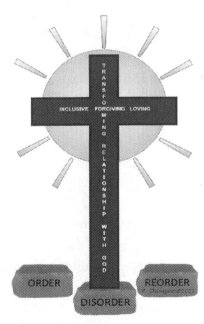

Figure 2: Depiction of the Spiritual Growth and
Transformational Journey in Christ

I will explain the symbolism and meaning behind the depiction above. I would like to draw your attention to the two image groupings in the depiction above. The first grouping is the sun and the cross, which symbolizes the Trinity. The sun represents the cosmic creator (the Father). The rays of sun represent the Holy Spirit. Finally, the cross represents Christ Jesus. The second grouping is the cross with the three stones, which represents our journeys in Christ.

You will noticed that the cross is empty, indicating the "risen Christ," a symbol of resurrection. The vertical beam of the cross reaching up to the sun symbolizes our relationship to a cosmic, universal God. The horizontal beam reminds us of Jesus's outstretched arms on the cross, symbolizing his sacrifice and love for all of us, Christians and non-Christians alike. The cross is grounded on the rock of disorder. This reminds us that Jesus came to cause disorder to the order of his day and then reorder everything to show solidarity with us and God.

The three rocks—order, disorder, and reorder—represent the stages of spiritual growth and transformation. Order is the first stage of transformation or salvation. It is the stage where we feel innocent and safe. People in the order stage like the status quo and avoid change and the suffering that comes from change. They pretend that everything is good, even when it is not. Eventually, this ideal order breaks down and disappoints. It could be caused by the loss of a loved one, loss of a job, rejection by a friend, abuse by a parent, or a variety of life challenges. This is the beginning of the disorder stage, the second rock. Through these challenges, we lose part or all of our innocence and become wounded. We suffer. However, this is the stage where real growth and transformation can occur. This is the stage that makes us the most uncomfortable. Some people try to flee back to the first stage to avoid the pain and suffering, even if it kills them. We must go through the suffering in the disorder stage—not under, over, or around it. As with Jesus, we must suffer and die to be resurrected. The reorder stage, the third rock, is called, in various traditions, exodus, enlightenment, nirvana, heaven, salvation, or even resurrection. It is life after death. It is a new order in which we have let go of things that prevent us from building a transforming and loving relationship with God and our neighbors. We learn new ways to strength our relationships. We reflect on the wisdom we have gained and the price we have paid for it.

Experiencing the three stages of spiritual growth and transformation is not a one-time event. Rather, it is a cyclical pattern of spiritual growth and transformation that we take many, many times during our lives. It is what Christ Jesus has called us to do by asking us "to follow him."

I want to circle back and make further points regarding the cross. *Reality has a cruciform pattern.* The intersection of the cross represents cross-purposes, opposing contradictions, or polar views of reality. These include liberalism versus conservativism, democracy versus communism, pro-life versus pro-choice, or pro-gun rights versus pro-gun control. The cross intersection represents a dualistic view of reality. According to Rohr, "Jesus was killed in a collision of cross-purposes, conflicting interests, and half-truths, caught between the demands of an empire and the religious establishment of his day."[11] Jesus chose not to change the reality of the day. Rather he chose to live differently within his reality and within opposing contradictions. As Rohr writes, *"The best criticism of the bad is still the practice of the better."*[12] This living within the contradictions of reality is not without pain and suffering, as Jesus demonstrated. Jesus suffered and died because he chose to live within these opposing contradictions (i.e., disorder). He also demonstrated how to reorder through his resurrection. Jesus showed us how to follow him.

Written on the vertical beam of the cross is "Transforming Relationship with God." As shown in Figure 2, the vertical beam sits upon the rock of disorder. In the disorder state, we are exposed to our authentic states of being through acts of great love or great suffering— not through pious suffering, but "necessary" suffering. This is the state in which we see our true selves with God.

The following three words are written on the horizontal beam of the cross: inclusive, forgiving, and loving. These three words are key Christ-like behaviors that Jesus taught about and practiced throughout his life. We, as followers of Christ, are asked to *be inclusive, be forgiving,* and *be loving* toward all people, Christian and non-Christian alike.

The order of the three key behaviors is not arbitrary. *Forgiving* is placed at the intersection of the cross. As discussed earlier, the

---

[11]   Rohr, *The Universal Christ,* 147.
[12]   Rohr, *The Universal Christ,* 67.

intersection is where there are cross-purposes or opposing contradictions that provide opportunities for change and growth for us. The main theme of the cross is forgiveness, which was a radical idea taught and practiced by Jesus. Forgiveness is necessary and central to healing our spiritual and physical wounds and reconciling our relationships with others and God. Forgiveness may be the biggest action we take toward growing and transforming spiritually.

Being inclusive, another radical idea taught and practiced by Jesus, is intentionally placed first. Why? Because we first need to open and expand our minds beyond our Judeo-Christian eccentric thinking to a broader understanding of God and his creation. If we continue with the status quo, we remain tribal and exclusive with our faith and miss out on the invitation to be part of the true Body of Christ. Some people may argue that *being loving* should be first. I disagree. If we don't put inclusiveness and forgiveness before love, we only love the people we feel comfortable with. We don't grow spiritually or transform.

Being loving on the surface appears quite simply. We read in the Gospel of Mark, "And you shall love the Lord your God with all your heart and with all your soul and with all your mind and with all your strength. The second is this: 'You shall love your neighbor as yourself" (Mark 12:30–31 ESV). But what does this really mean? When we take a deeper look at what *being loving* means, we find it's not so clear or simple. The definition of love tends to be more of abstract than actionable. I was not satisfied with the definition of love, so I created my own actionable definition for love. Here is my definition of being loved.

One who feels truly heard, affirmed, and treated with dignity, feels valued.

One who feels valued, feels loved.

I want to provide a deeper understanding of this definition. First, it is implied that the two people are in the present moment and not distracted with things around them or thoughts of the day. "Truly heard" means that the listener pays attention and hears what the person is saying without judging or giving advice. The listener paraphrases back to the person what he or she has heard and asks clarifying questions if necessary. "Truly affirmed" means that the person listening shows emotional support and encouragement towards the person without condoning bad behavior or necessarily agreeing with him or her. Remember, we all were created in the image of God and we all are sinners at times. "Treated with dignity" means that the listener shows that the person is worthy of respect. If the person feels that he or she has received these three things, the person feels valued. If the person feels valued, he or she usually feels loved to some degree.

This type of love is actionable. It can be given to anyone, even your enemies. This love builds relationships and mutual understanding across differences, religious traditions, political boundaries, races, and genders. This type of love leads to the *broader community's* transformation in Christ.

It is my hope that you have a better understanding of the spiritual growth and transformation journey in Christ. I hope you will find it helpful.

CHAPTER 4

CHARTING THE SPIRITUAL JOURNEY

I believe our spiritual journeys are more analogous to sailing across the sea than climbing mountains. There is no road map to heaven or spiritual transformation in spite of what religious tradition would tell you. There is no direct path to salvation.

Each of us comes into the world from different parents, genders, races, nationalities, religious traditions, and life experiences. We each start in different places. No one lives exactly the same. We all have the freedom to make choices and see the world from different views. We behave differently based on our life experiences. Therefore, to believe that there is a road map for salvation is very naive, very simplistic.

The spiritual journey is more like sailing a boat on the sea. There are no maps for sailors to navigate the sea; rather, they use nautical charts. Sailors use the nautical charts to prepare and chart their courses to their desired destinations. Typically, the planned courses to their destinations are not straight ones. There are conditions to contend with, such as wind direction and speed, weather, tides, and water hazards. The sailor must consider all of these conditions when plotting or charting his or her course. These sailing conditions cause sailors to deviate from the true straight-line course. If sailing conditions were not enough, sailors must adjust their directional readings based on the deviation between their compass readings and true north. Each nautical chart has a compass rose that shows this deviation. An example of a compass rose is shown in Figure 3.

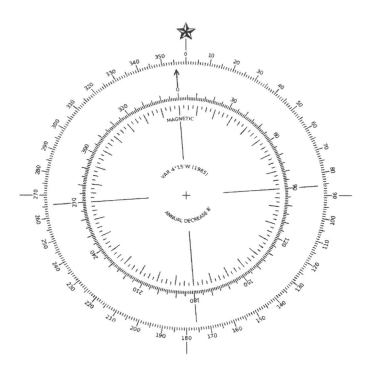

Figure 3: Example of a Compass Rose

Sailors use magnetic compasses, which point to the magnetic north, to navigate their courses when sailing. Nautical charts are based on true north. Sailors must adjust the nautical chart readings of their planned courses to their compass readings. Compass readings are what sailors use when sailing their boats. To add another layer of complexity, the variation between true north and magnetic north changes based on your location on the earth. Therefore, sailors need to know their locations in order to use the correct variation adjustment. Sailors may decide to plan some stops along their journeys. Those stops must be added to their chart plans.

Once the chart plans are completed, sailors need to decide if they are sailing alone or with a crew. If they decide on a crew, they must decide how many and what skills they need. Next, the sailors need to estimate what supplies they will need and how much. Too many supplies makes the boat heavy, slow, and hard to maneuver. Too few supplies mean sailors and crew may starve before getting to a destination.

Finally, sailors start their journeys with the guide of their chart plans. Sailors must adjust their chart plans as conditions change. Deviation from a plan may be due to unexpected weather or a water hazard. It may happen due to inexperienced crew or careless captains. A chart plan helps to identify the unexpected and enables sailors to regain their courses.

The sailing analogy is similar to our spiritual journeys in Christ. Most Christians would say that heaven is their final destination, which is true. However, heaven is not a place, but a state of being. Our final destinations or goals are to find and be our true selves in Christ. When we pass from this earth, we become united with Christ—fully human and divine like Christ. This is heaven.

In keeping with the sailing analogy, Christians are not given nautical charts for their spiritual journeys. Yes, we hear stories of other people's spiritual journeys through the Bible, accounts of the saints, and accounts from ordinary people. However, we are never shown or give nautical charts for our journeys. Some of us are like Christopher Columbus, sailing off for the new world without any charts or sense of direction and becoming lost.

Our religious traditions provide us with some direction, like the magnetic north for sailors, to start our spiritual journeys. However, a religious tradition, like the magnetic north, is not the true God (i.e., true north), but rather a variation from it. As with the magnetic north pole, religious traditions around the world vary from the true God. Our religious traditions, like a magnet north, draw us toward seeking God. However, religious traditions do not always direct us to the true God.

For most of us, our religious traditions are starting places for our spiritual journeys. For Christians, we learned about God through church teachings, doctrine, and practices. The church taught us how to behave through reward and punishment. For the last 2000 years, church authority has been more concerned on the size of your boat, how well you follow the boating rules, who you pick for crew members, and how and where you operate your boat. For them, it has never been about your spiritual journey. Yet, this is the spiritual journey of the Christian Church. It is growing in Christ as we are, with all its imperfections and contradictions. Like us, the church is a work in progress. According to Rohr, "The best criticism of the bad is still the practice of the better."[13]

Is there such a thing like a nautical chart for your spiritual journey? Yes, it is ancient tool called the Enneagram. The Enneagram has been traced to a fourth-century Desert Father by the name of Evagrius Ponticus and was passed orally through the Islamic wisdom tradition of Sufism. Some speculate that the Enneagram dates back to Pythagoras, a Greek philosopher and mathematician. Rohr and Ebert write that the "Enneagram was probably used for centuries to help spiritual directors train and refine the gift of 'the reading of souls' and transforming of people into who they are in God."[14] At a high level, the Enneagram is another typology tool, like the Myers-Briggs Type Indicator that describes personality types. However, the Enneagram goes beyond describing personality traits within the common personality groups. Its inner dynamic is about bringing on change or conversion in a person through self-awareness and self-knowledge. The Enneagram helps a person uncover those thoughts and actions that hide his or her true self. It uncovers the good, the bad, and the ugly within us. I will expand on the Enneagram in the Chapter 5.

The Enneagram test can be taken online. I recommend the Enneagram Institute. The Riso-Hudson Enneagram Type Indicator (RHETI) is a forced-choice personality test that has been scientifically validated and is comprised of 144 paired statements. It costs $12 to take. Here is the link: https://tests.enneagraminstitute.com/. The Riso-Hudson's nine Enneagram type descriptors are shown in Figure 4 below.

---

[13]   Rohr, *The Universal Christ*, 67.
[14]   Richard Rohr and Andreas Ebert, *The Enneagram: A Christian Perspective* (New York: The Crossroad Publishing Company, 2016), 22.

The Peacemaker
9
The Challenger 8   1 The Reformer
The Enthusiast 7   2 The Helper
The Loyalist 6   3 The Achiever
5   4
The Investigator   The Individualist

Figure 4: Riso-Hudson's Nine Enneagram Type Descriptors

Like sailors, we will need knowledge and skills to sail our boats. Each of us was born with original goodness and received innate knowledge of God through each of our spiritual beings. Your spiritual being is made up of two parts: the conscious mind (what poets and musicians refer to as the "soul") and the spirit, the vibrational energy that the body emits and that connects you with God. Everything—humans, animals, plants, rocks, and so on—has a spirit. Only humans have spirits and souls.

Your soul is made up of the rational mind and the emotional heart. The emotional heart communicates to you through your *feelings and emotions* and is connected to your inner voice of intuitive knowing. Unfortunately, many of us have been trained to believe that feelings and emotions are not to be trusted. Your feelings and emotions are neither good or bad—they just are. Your emotions and feelings are your internal sensors that sense the conditions around and within you. The interpretation of feelings and emotions by the mind can lead to either constructive or destructive actions. The feelings and emotions are just sensory information, like information provided by a thermometer. How you react to the temperature reading is based on your interpretation of past experiences. Through the practice of contemplative prayer, which will be explained in the next chapter, you will be able to develop a healthy emotional heart and inner voice.

As sailors use compasses to help navigate their boats in the right direction, we use contemplative prayer, along with our prayer postures, to navigate us in the right direction to our true selves and the true God. Contemplative prayer and prayer postures will be discussed in the next chapter.

For sailors, a ship's log is used to record future and current weather and sea conditions, current operating conditions of the ship, and any observations that could aid in navigation and safe passage along their journeys. A spiritual journal is much the same. In your journal, you record your thoughts, decisions, and actions on your current and future realities and relationships, your assessment of your mind, body, and spirit, and any next steps on your journey.

Summary comparison between taking a sailing voyage and a spiritual journey is tabulated in Table 2.

Sailboat	Spiritual
Sailboat Captain	You
Sailboat	Your human body
Boat Cargo	Your soul and spirit
Nautical Chart	Your Enneagram results
Compass	Contemplative prayer with your prayer posture
Compass Rose	Variance between the true God and our churchly interpretation of God
Crew	Your faith community
Supplies	The Eucharist

CHAPTER 5

THE ENNEAGRAM

A t first, your impressions of the Enneagram most likely will be that the Enneagram is just a caricature of your personality. The English word *personality* is derived from the Latin word for "mask."[15] Your personality is shaped by your ego. *Ego* is defined as the view that a person has of himself or herself. The word ego comes from the Latin word for I. Another common definition for ego is a person's self-esteem or self-importance. Through the use of the Enneagram, you will uncover the masks that your ego has created to hide your true self from you. As you delve deeper into understanding the Enneagram, you will find that it is quite dynamic and can bring about change or conversion in a person through self-awareness and self-knowledge. In other words, your personality is not fixed, but is ever changing based on your insights and actions.

As Christopher L. Huertz explains, "Enneagram offers a sacred map for our souls; a map that when understood, leads us home to our true identity and to God."[16] The Enneagram explains the "why" of how we think, feel, and act. The other aspect of the Enneagram is that it answers the questions "Who am I?" (identity) and "What am I worth?" (dignity).

---

[15] Christopher L. Heuertz, *The Sacred Enneagram, Finding Your Unique Path to Spiritual Growth* (Grand Rapids, MI: Zondervan, 2017), 30.

[16] Huertz, *The Sacred Enneagram*, 26.

In the United States at least, we believe our identities come from *what we have, what we do,* or *what other people say or think about us.* Chris Sugden calls them the three human lies about ourselves.[17] However, as Christians, we are all born with original goodness and given intrinsic dignity from God. Therefore, dignity assumes identity. The Enneagram helps us uncover these three lies in us so we can confront them and discover our true selves.

The word Enneagram is derived from the Greek words *ennea* meaning nine and *gramma* meaning sign or figure. The Enneagram figure is pictured in Figure 5. Father Richard Rohr and Andreas Ebert, in their book *The Enneagram: A Christian Perspective,* prefer to use the type's number when describing a type as opposed to using a label. A label tends add to the perception that the Enneagram is a personality caricature and fixed. Instead, each type's description has depth and breath. In addition, the type's description is not black or white. It is like a rainbow with different shades of color. As you become more familiar in using the Enneagram, you will discover that your inner self is not so black and white, but, like a rainbow, made up of shades of color.

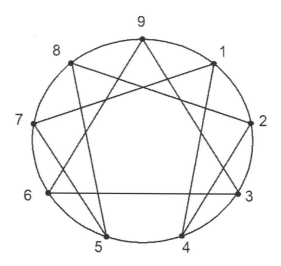

17   Chris Sugden, *Seeking the Asian Face of Jesus: The Practice and Theology of Christian Social Witness in Indonesia and India 1974–1996* (Oxford, UK: Regnum, 1997), 183.

Figure 5: The Enneagram

The nine types are arranged around a circle at a distance of 45 degrees from each other. The circle denotes eternity, unity, wholeness, and inclusivity of all things—*the Law of One*. The equilateral triangle represents what is know as the *Law of Three*—the three forces that guide everything in motion: active, passive and neutral. The equilateral triangle also represents the Trinity. The irregular, crisscrossed six pointed hexagram with the Enneagram circle is used to teach the *Law of Seven*.[18] The Law of Seven is thought to explain the spectrum of all things like light (refracted through the seven colors of the rainbow), sound (heard through the seven fundamental tones of an octave), sequence (the seven days of the week forming the basic interval of time), and energy (the seven Chakras of body's energy centers that yoga students learn).[19]

Let's take a deeper look into the symbolism behind the Enneagram figure. For Pythagoras, numbers were used for more than just counting and calculation. Numbers had mystical meaning. In case of the Enneagram, which is our nautical chart to seek out Christ, the numbers seven and ten are significant. Seven (7) symbolizes completeness and perfection in both the physical and spiritual sense. Seven represents Jesus Christ. The number ten (10) symbolizes total completion, perfection, and harmony under God's authority and order. Ten represents God's new covenant through Jesus's suffering and dying to show God's outpouring love for us. Adding seven and ten together, we get seventeen. The meaning of seventeen is that of "overcoming the enemy" and "complete victory." Seventeen represents Jesus's victory over death. The

---

[18] The six sides of the hexagon plus the circle makes seven. The hexagon within the circle symbolizes the six days that God created heaven and earth and on the seven day (holy day), he rested.

[19] Huertz, *The Sacred Enneagram*, 40–42.

Enneagram contains three equilateral triangles (9-3-6-9, 8-2-5-8, and 7-1-4-7). If the number seventeen is taken as the side of an equilateral triangle, the total sum of the sides of the three equilateral triangles is 153. In John's Gospel, we are told how after his resurrection, Jesus saw his disciples casting their fishing nets into the Sea of Genesareth. He ordered them to throw their nets into the sea on the right side of the boat. They obeyed and caught 153 large fish. In the sixth century, St. Jerome interpreted the number of fish as the grand total of 153 species of fish at the time of Jesus. The number 153 denotes the universality and inclusion of all people into the body of Christ. The Enneagram is a tool for all people seeking spiritual growth and transformation in Christ. The Enneagram has a mystical quality.

The nine types (or nine ways) of the Enneagram form a sort of color wheel that describes the basic archetype of humanity's tragic flaws, sin tendencies, primary fears, and unconscious needs.[20] An archetype is defined as the personification of a collection of human attributes that defines a certain human character, like *the hero*.

The nine types of the Enneagram have the following common attributes: mirrors, needs, holy ideas, virtues, fixations, passions, intelligence centers, basic desires, and basic fears. The characteristics for the nine attributes by Enneagram type are tabulated in Table 1. The characteristics should not be viewed as black or white, like labels or descriptors. Rather, they are color gradients where colors transition from one to the other like a rainbow. For example, Nines tend to be lazy, but not all the time or to the same degree. Difference experiences and situations demonstrate Nines' laziness in different ways and at different intensities. Nines need to reflect on how their laziness has manifested itself in the situation and learn from the experience.

The Enneagram offers nine mirrors for self-reflection (column two in Table 1). These nine mirrors can help us remove the masks that get in the way of seeing our true selves and from going home.

---

20   Huertz, *The Sacred Enneagram*, 49.

Each of the nine types has a central need, as displayed in column three in Table 1.

Each of the nine types has its Holy Idea and Virtue as tabulated in columns four and five in Table 1. As Christopher Huertz writes, the

> Holy Idea, "column four," of the each type is the *mental clarity* of the True Self that emerges when the mind is at rest, while Virtue, "column five," of each type is the *emotional objectivity* of the True Self that comes forward in a heart is at peace. Together, our Holy idea and Virtue express who were always created to be.[21]

Earlier, in Chapter 2, I introduced you to the belief that we are all born with original goodness and given intrinsic dignity from God. As children, we learn how to have our needs and desires met, either by trial and error or mimicking others, such as our parents. We quickly learn how to receive what we want in the fastest way. When we, as children, don't get what we want or someone hurts us, we feel hurt and anger— we feel wounded. Through our wounded experiences, we formulate our own perceptions of the world and develop means to cope with the world and get what we want. As children, we are very self-centered. How we cope or get our needs met as children is not necessarily considerate or loving at times to others. As we mature, we develop sin-tendencies, our main "go-to actions," when we are hurt or desire something. Our sin-tendencies have two parts: our reactions to how we see and think about the world (fixations) and our reactions to how we feel about the world around us (passions). For example, Type Ones may believe that "life should be fair." Life is not fair all the time, which makes Ones resentful—this is their fixation. Ones feel hurt and ignored when they perceive a situation as unfair. Ones react by showing their anger towards others—this is their passion. Our egos justify our sinful behaviors to preserve the false selves, which in turn hides our true selves and cut

---

21   Huertz, *The Sacred Enneagram*, 36.

us off from God. The fixations and passions for the nine types are tabulated in columns six and seven in Table 1.

The nine types are divided among three groups, which are referred to as Intelligence Centers. The Intelligence Centers are the basis for how we perceive ourselves in relationship to our understanding of how the world works and how we work in the world.[22] The Intelligence Centers include the Body (instinctive or gut) Center, the Heart (feeling or emotion) Center, and the Head (mind, thinking, or rational) Center. Each of these Intelligence Centers offers us a different way of experiencing the loving presence and voice of God. As we become more aware and leverage our Intelligence Centers, we become better at spiritual discernment. Spiritual discernment is a decision-making process in which an individual allows God to help in making a discovery that can lead to future action. The three Intelligence Centers with their corresponding Enneagram types are displayed in Figure 6. Your dominant type will determine which Intelligence Center you belong to.

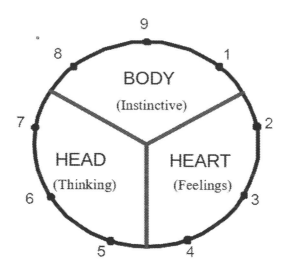

Figure 6: Nine Types by Intelligence Center

The Intelligence Centers explain something about each of the nine Enneagram Types by helping identify a person's most *accessible*

---

22   Huertz, *The Sacred Enneagram*, 90.

emotional response or reaction: *anxiety or distress* for the Head Center, *fear and shame* for the Heart Center, and *frustration or anger* for the Body Center.[23] Our Intelligence Centers are how God speaks to us. We must learn to trust what our Intelligence Centers tell us. That is the purpose of spiritual discernment. For a further understanding of each Intelligence Center, I direct you to Chapter 4 in Chris Heuertz's book *The Sacred Enneagram: Finding Your Unique Path to Spiritual Growth.*

Knowing our Intelligence Centers and matching them to the appropriate contemplative prayer postures will allow us to spiritually align and grow in Christ. Contemplative prayer is prayer in which we seek being more intimate and in union with God (i.e., loving God). In contrast, centering prayer is a receptive, silent prayer in which we express our desire to invite God into our spaces (i.e., consenting to God). The three contemplative prayer postures are silence, stillness, and solitude. Their relation to the Intelligence Centers is shown in Figure 7.

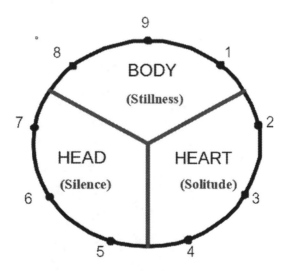

Figure 7: The Three Contemplative Prayer Postures
with Their Corresponding Intelligence Centers

---

23   Huertz, *The Sacred Enneagram*, 91.

Table: The Characteristics of the Nine Attributes by Enneagram Type[24]

Type	Mirrors	Needs	Holy Ideas	Virtues	Fixations	Passions	Intelligence Centers	Basic Desires	Basic Fears
One	Strives for principled excellence as moral duty	The Need to be Perfect	Perfection	Serenity	Resentment	Anger	Body (Gut)	To be good, to have integrity	Of being bad, imbalanced, defective, corrupt
Two	Strives for lavish love through self-sacrifice	The Need to Be Needed	Will, Freedom	Humility	Flattery	Pride	Heart (Feeling)	To feel love	Of being unloved
Three	Strives for appreciation recognition through curated successes	The Need to Succeed	Harmony, Hope	Truthfulness, Authenticity	Vanity	Deceit	Heart (Feeling)	To feel valuable	Of being worthless, without inherent value
Four	Strives for the discovery of identity for faithful authenticity	The Need to Be Special (or Unique)	Origin	Equanimity, Emotional Balance	Melancholy (Pensive Sadness)	Envy	Heart (Feeling)	To be themselves	Of having no identity or significance
Five	Strives for decisive clarity through thoughtful conclusions	The Need to Perceive (or Understand)	Transparency	Detachment	Stinginess	Avarice (Excessive Greediness)	Head (Thinking)	To be capable and competent	Of being helpless, incompetent, and incapable
Six	Strives for steady constancy through confident loyalty	The Need to Be Sure/Certain (or Secure)	Strength, Faith (Trust)	Courage	Cowardice	Fear	Head (Thinking)	To have support and guidance	Of being without support and guidance
Seven	Strives for imaginative freedom for inspirational independence	The Need to Avoid Pain	Wisdom	Sobriety	Planning	Gluttony	Head (Thinking)	To be satisfied	Of being trapped in pain and deprivation
Eight	Strives for impassioned intensity for unfettered autonomy	The Need to Be Against	Truth	Innocence	Vengeance	Lust	Body (Gut)	To protect themselves	Of being harmed, controlled and violated
Nine	Strives for harmonious peacefulness as congruent repose	The Need to Avoid	Love	Action	Indolence (Laziness)	Sloth	Body (Gut)	To have peace of mind and wholeness	Of being lost, separated and fragmented

---

24   Huertz, *The Sacred Enneagram,* 29, 35, 36, 38, 74, 75, 90–91, and 111–112.

The prayer posture for the Head Center is silence: silencing the mind to hear the presence of God. For the Heart Center, the prayer posture is solitude: being alone with God and feeling his presence. For the Body Center, the prayer posture is stillness: being still to sense the presence of God. Here are the steps to contemplative prayer.

1. Create a sacred space that is quiet and where you won't be disturbed. Set up a small table and a comfortable chair. Make your sacred place your own. You may want decorate it with candles, religious artifacts, flowers, incense, and so on. You want your sacred space to help set the mood to be in God's presence. You will need a small box with a lid. I will explain its use later.

   I encourage you to bless your sacred space with holy water and incense using the following prayer.

   > Holy cosmic source of being, one who sent Jesus, the cosmic Christ, to model the true path of transformation by suffering, dying, and resurrecting through his passion and cross, send the cosmic Spirit to cleanse and bless my sacred space. Make this space safe for me to explore my deepest inner being and unmask my false self so that I may discover my true self and take action toward transforming myself in Christ. I ask this in the name of the Father, Son, and Holy Spirit. Amen.

2. Go to your sacred place wearing comfortable clothes. Turn off your cell phone. Sit and light a candle. Open the empty box on your table. Take a few minutes and identify and write on piece of paper those things that are at the top of mind for today. Review them, place them in the empty box, and close the box. You can retrieve them later. Now it's time to live in the moment with God's presence.

3. Formulate a focus statement and say it out loud. Try to be specific if possible. For example, *I want to explore and understand why I am so resentful at times with certain people at work.*

4. Next, quiet yourself and close your eyes. Start by sensing your surroundings, like the temperature of your sacred space and any sounds, like air movement, birds chirping, or traffic noise. Slowly concentrate and be aware of any body sensations, such as muscle tension or pain, and any feelings, such as anxiety, happiness, worry, sadness, or gratefulness. Next concentrate on your breathing. Slowly inhale through your noise. Feel the air fill your lungs. Exhale through your mouth. Feel how the air leaves your lungs and mouth. Concentrate on your breathing for about five minutes

5. After your breathing has become deep and rhythmic, implement your prayer posture: Head people should be silent, Heart people should be in solitude, and Body people should be still. Concentrate on your breathing and prayer posture. If your thoughts of the day interrupt your contemplative prayer, acknowledge them and let them go. Return to your breathing and your focus statement. Note your emotions, thoughts, and how your body feels. Continue your contemplative prayer for fifteen to twenty minutes.

    At first, your thoughts will interrupt your prayer a lot. This is normal for everyone starting out. Be patient with yourself. It takes time and practice. Eventually, you will reach a deep inner peace and feel the presence of God. From your prayer posture, God will communicate with you.

6. After fifteen to twenty minutes, slowly open your eyes. Take a deep breath and exhale. Slowly become aware of your surroundings. Then say this prayer of gratitude.

    Thank you, cosmic Spirit for sitting with me today
    as I contemplate my spiritual and physical wounds,
    my shadow side, and my sins that inhibit my
    spiritual journey. Thank you for pointing out my

goodness—my true self. Thank you for comforting me as I re-experience the pain and suffering from my childhood wounds. Thank you for being here in union with Christ Jesus and the cosmic Creator. Amen.

7. Close your contemplative prayer session with the following prayer: Go in the peace of Christ Jesus. In the name of the cosmic Creator, the Christ Jesus, and the cosmic Spirit. Amen.
8. Write any thoughts, feelings, or sensations from your prayer session in your spiritual journal.

A few additional thoughts about the spiritual journal. The spiritual journal is a very important tool for your journey. It is a great place to capture your feelings, thoughts, reactions, decisions, outcomes, and actions throughout your day so they may be contemplated and reflected on later. It is great place to record your spiritual wounds from others and the wounds you inflict on others. Your journal is great place to capture your thoughts on and reactions to what you learn from your Enneagram. Your journal doesn't have to be well written. It only has to be written well enough for you to understand it. The hardest part about writing a journal is starting a journal—so start!

To finish the discussion on the nine attributes of the nine Enneagram types, the characteristics of the Basic Desire (column 9) and Basic Fear (column 10) are tabulated in Table 10. Basic Desire is the ego's desire to seek our original goodness—our true selves. Basic Fear is our ego's compulsive fear that prevents us from seeking our true selves.

The types on either side of your dominant type are referred to as your wings. Throughout your life, you may borrow characteristics from your wing type. For example, I am a Type 6 and have a tendency to be risk adverse. When I develop scenarios to reach a desired outcome, I borrow characteristics from Type 5, *analysis and objectivity*, to ensure my plans are balanced between risk and reward. A balanced plan opens up new opportunities that a risk adverse Type 6 would never entertain.

The crisscrossed lines in the Enneagram diagram show the

movements of our types when operating in healthy or unhealthy states. I adopted the Enneagram Institute's classification of the lines as either Integration (a move toward a healthy state) or Disintegration (a move toward an unhealthy state). The Integration and Disintegration lines of the Enneagram are displayed in Figure 8.[25] The Enneagram Institute explains the nine levels of development from Level 1, the most healthy state, to Level 9, the most unhealthy state. If you take the test from the Enneagram Institute, you will receive a full explanation of the nine levels of development. For example, a healthy person dominant in Type 6 integrates or borrows some of the positive traits from Type 9, like trusting. This allows a Type 6 to relax his or her hyper-vigilance and be himself or herself. It is important to note that we do not *become* the types we integrate toward. We merely reach across and borrow positive traits to integrate into healthier dominant types.

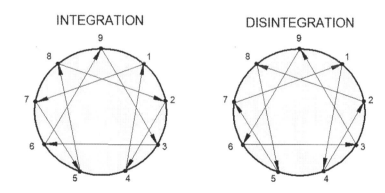

Figure 8: Integration and Disintegration Lines of the Enneagram

In contrast, the subconscious self-preservation instinct of an unhealthy person dominant in Type 6 borrows some of the traits from Type 3, like being *excessively driven*, to prevent falling farther down into unhealthiness. Sixes are often anxious at work, react to self-doubt, and become caught in over-thinking a problem. If stress escalates beyond normal levels, Sixes jump into action, trying to deal with their anxiety by working harder. It is to be understood that the dominant type does not consciously borrow negative traits from the disintegrating type.

---

25   Huertz, *The Sacred Enneagram*, 65.

The intent of this section was to give you a high-level understanding of the Enneagram and how it can be used for self-discovery and spiritual growth.

I have added the Enneagram types to my depiction as shown in Figure 9 below

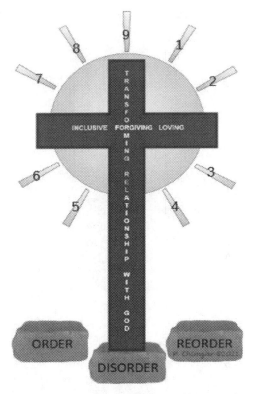

Figure 9: Depiction of the Spiritual Growth and Transformational Journey in Christ

CHARTER 6

FINAL THOUGHTS

I began this book by sharing my faith journey, my childhood wounds, and my struggle with mental illness. I learned that my journey in faith was not the same as my spiritual journey. My faith journey was about "knowing" and growing in a religious tradition, in my case, Roman Catholicism. It was more about becoming a loyal, informed, and practicing Catholic. I felt that the Catholic Church was more concerned about individual behavior management than spiritual growth and transformation of the individual and community.

After reading Father Rohr's book, *The Universal Christ*, I had a paradigm shift in my religious and spiritual beliefs. I came to believe the following.

- I was born of original goodness and not original sin.
- Jesus Christ died to show God's outpouring love for us. Through his resurrection, he has transformed us into the Body of Christ.
- Jesus punishes no one, but forgives and includes everyone, Christians and non-Christians alike.
- *Sin* is a deviation from Christ's paths for us and can be opportunities of spiritual growth if we learn from the lesson.

- There is a loving, forgiving God, who is a universal, cosmic God that includes all things and loves all things, not just earthlings.
- Our spiritual journeys are about spiritually growing and transforming in Christ as individuals and within communities.

I learned that my spiritual journey was about unmasking my ego, which has hidden my true self from others and myself. I learned that I needed to be brave and honest with myself to face the good, the bad, and the ugly in myself. I learned that God loves all of me and not just when I am "good."

I learned that there are three stages of transformation in Christ: *order, disorder,* and *reorder.* Together, these stages make up the process for my spiritual journey that I have been seeking. I found that the stages of spiritual transformation were rooted in early Christian thinking.

I learned that I needed to focus and practice the three Christ like behaviors towards others by being inclusive, forgiving, and loving. I need to advocate for and practice restorative justice, as Jesus did.

I learned about the Enneagram and how it could be used to chart my course on my spiritual journey.

Lastly, I constructed the following depiction to help remind me of all that I have learned and having a way of sharing my spiritual journey with others.

I am grateful that you took the time to read this book. Thank you. My hope is that this book will encourage you on your spiritual journey to seek your true self in Christ. God Bless.

INCLUSIVE FORGIVING LOVING

TRANSFORMING RELATIONSHIP WITH GOD

ORDER

DISORDER

REORDER

P. Chinger ©2021

BIBLIOGRAPHY

Baars, Conrad W. and Anna A. Terruwe. *Healing the Unaffirmed, Recognizing Emotional Deprivation Disorder.* New York: Society of St. Paul, 2002.

Heuertz, Christopher L. *The Sacred Enneagram, Finding Your Unique Path to Spiritual Growth.* Grand Rapids, MI: Zondervan, 2017.

Kiprop, Victor. "How Long Have Humans Been On Earth?" World Atlas. Accessed January 12 2021. https://www.worldatlas.com/articles/how-long-have-humans-been-on-earth.html.

Rohr, Richard, and Andreas Ebert. *The Enneagram: A Christian Perspective*, New York: The Crossroad Publishing Company, 2016.

Rohr, Richard. *Universal Christ: How a Forgotten Reality Can Change Everything We See, Hope For, and Believe.* New York: Convergent Books, 2019.

Sugden, Chris. *Seeking the Asian Face of Jesus: The Practice and Theology of Christian Social Witness in Indonesia and India 1974–1996.* Oxford, UK: Regnum, 1997.

Printed in the United States
by Baker & Taylor Publisher Services